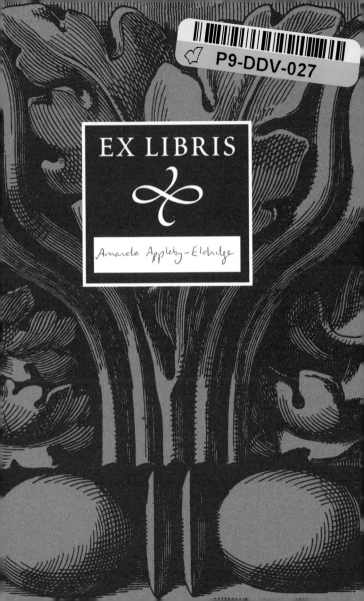

EX LIBRIS

*Amanda Appleby-Eldridge*

P9-DDV-027

# NOTA BENE

# Nota Bene

## A Guide to Familiar Latin Quotes and Phrases

EDITED BY
Robin Langley Sommer

BARNES
&NOBLE
BOOKS
NEW YORK

✥

IN MEMORIAM
MARYELLEN ABLEY

✥

Produced by DoveTail Books

Copyright © 1995, DoveTail Books
Design copyright © Ziga Design

This edition published by Barnes & Noble, Inc.
by arrangement with DoveTail books

1995 Barnes & Noble Books

All rights reserved. No part of this publication
may be reproduced, stored in a retrieval system or transmitted
in any form by any means, electronic, mechanical, photocopying
or otherwise, without first obtaining the written permission
of the copyright owner.

ISBN 0-7607-0079-6

Printed in China

7  9  8  6

# Contents

# Foreword

*N*ow that the study of classical languages has become less common than it was a hundred years ago, many educated English-speaking people welcome a succinct guide to the Latin roots of their language. Perhaps half of all English words in current use are of Latin origin, and it is inseparable from the study of the Romance languages: French, Italian, Spanish, Portuguese, and Romanian. In addition, the great writers of Roman civilization have left their imprint on these living languages in the form of quotations, maxims, anecdotes, figures of speech, and ideas that are still germane and powerful almost 2000 years later. Through all its phases of development, from the preliterary Latin of ancient Italy through the Medieval Latin of European schools and monasteries that preserved the classical heritage, Latin has endured as a language of rare beauty and precision, coloring our lives in ways we may not even be aware of. In the realm of language, all roads do, indeed, lead to Rome.

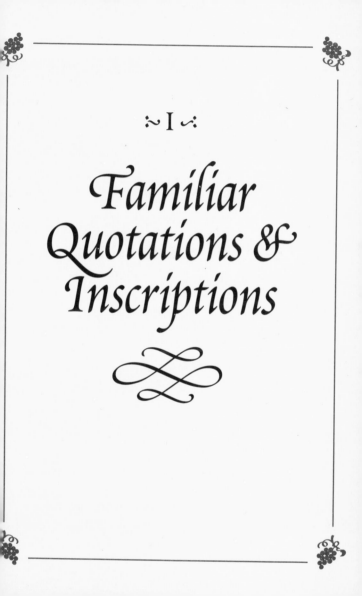

~ I ~

# Familiar Quotations & Inscriptions

# Idioms: Latin Everyone Knows

### Ad hoc
For this particular purpose
(common usage: improvise)

### Ad captandum vulgus
To appeal to the crowd

### Ad hominem
To the person (to appeal to feelings
rather than reason)

### Ad libitum (ad lib)
Freely; at pleasure

### Alea iacta est
The die is cast

### Alter ego
Another self

### Amicus curiae
Friend of the court (objective adviser)

### Ars gratia artis
Art for art's sake

### Ars longa, vita brevis
Art is long, life is short

### Bona fide
In good faith

### Carpe diem
Sieze the day
(make the most of the opportunity)

### Cave canem
Beware of the dog!

### Caveat emptor
Let the buyer beware

### *Ceteris paribus*
Other things being equal

### *Circa*
About, approximately

### *Cogito ergo sum*
I think, therefore I am
(Descartes, *seventeenth century*)

### *Cui bono*
Whom does it benefit?

### *Cum grano salis*
With a grain of salt

### *De novo*
Anew

### *Deus ex machina*
An improbable solution, artificially introduced
to resolve a difficulty or untangle a dramatic plot

*Divide et impera*
Divide and rule

*E pluribus unum*
From many, one

*Ecce homo*
Behold the man!

*Emeritus*
Honorary; by reason of merit

*Errare humanum est*
To err is human

*Ex animo*
From the heart; sincerely

*Ex libris*
From the books of
(from the library of)

*Ex post facto*
After the fact

*Fortes fortuna juvat*
Fortune favors the brave

*Hic jacet* _____
Here lies _____

*Habeas corpus*
A legal writ to end unlawful restraint
by bringing a prisoner into court

*In memoriam*
In memory of

*In toto*
Altogether

*In vino veritas*
In wine is truth

**Lapsus linguae**
A slip of the tongue

**Lapsus memoriae**
A slip of the memory

**Magna cum laude**
With great honor

**Magnum opus**
Masterpiece (a great work)

**Mea culpa**
My fault

**Mens sana in corpore sano**
Sound of body, sound of mind

**Mirabile dictu**
Wonderful to tell

*Multum in parvo*
Much in a little

*Naturo abhorret a vacuo*
Nature abhors a vacuum

*Nolens volens*
Whether willing or not (willy-nilly)

*Noli me tangere*
Let nothing touch me (do not interfere)

*Non compos mentis*
Of unsound mind

*Non sequitur*
A statement that does not follow
logically from what preceded it

*Omnia vincit amor*
Love conquers all

*Pax vobiscum*
Peace be with you

*Per annum*
Per year

*Per capita*
Per head

*Pro bono publico*
For the public good

*Pro tempore*
For the time being
(temporarily)

*Persona non grata*
An unpleasing person

*Quid pro quo*
A thing for a thing (substitute)

*Quieta non movere*
Do not move settled things
(let sleeping dogs lie)

*Sapere aude*
Dare to be wise

*Status quo*
The existing state of affairs

*Summum bonum*
The supreme good

*Summum ius summa inuria*
The more law, the less justice

*Tabula rasa*
A clean slate

*Terra firma*
Solid ground

*Terra incognita*
An unknown land

*Usus est magister optimus*
Practice makes perfect

*Via*
By way of

*Via media*
The middle path

*Vice versa*
With the order or
meaning reversed

*Vox populi, vox dei*
The voice of the people is
the voice of God

# Familiar Mottoes

### Ave Atque Vale
Hail and Farewell!

### De Mortuis Nil Nisi Bonum
Let Nothing But Good Be Said of the Dead

### Dominus Illuminatio Mea
May the Lord Guide Me

### Dum Spiro, Spero
While I Breathe, I Hope

### Esto Perpetua
It Is Everlasting

### Excelsior
Ever Upward!

### Labor Omnia Vincit
Labor Conquers All Things

*Justitia Omnibus*
Justice to All

*Nil Sine Numini*
Nothing Without Providence

*Per Ardua Ad Astra*
Through Hardship to the Stars

*Regnat Populus*
The People Rule

*Semper Fidelis*
Always Faithful

*Semper Paratus*
Always Prepared

*Sic Semper Tyrannis*
Thus Always to Tyrants

# Expressions from Roman Drama

## Plautus (ca. 251–184 BC)

### A WORD TO THE WISE

**SATURIO** Here I am! Hope I didn't keep you waiting.
**TOXILUS** Go on, get over there far off and out of sight,
   and be silent;
  When you see me talking to the pimp—
  A word to the wise is enough.

—*THE PERSIAN*, ACT 4, SC. 7, li. 726–27

### WHOM THE GODS LOVE DIES YOUNG

**CHRYSALUS** Whom the gods love
  Dies young; yet he lives—breathes—is conscious.
  If any god loved this man, he should have died
  More than ten, no, more than twenty years ago.
  He burdens the ground as he walks, already senseless
  And witless, worth about as much as a stinking
  mushroom.

—*THE TWO BACCHISES*, ACT 4, SC. 7, li. 816–821

## Terence (ca. 195–159 BC)

### FORTUNE FAVORS THE BRAVE

**ANTIPHO** Wretched me! How can I find a remedy for
this sudden ruin?
For if it is my fortune, Phanium, to be divided
from you,
Life is no longer desirable to me.

**GETA** Now that it is so, Antipho,
So much the more ought you be watchful: fortune
favors the brave.

—*PHORMIO*, ACT I, SC. 3, li. 201–203

### NOTHING IS SAID THAT HAS
### NOT BEEN SAID BEFORE

He doesn't deny that in his *Eunuch* he has transported
characters out of the Greek; but…if the same characters
will not be permitted, how is it more permissible to depict
a servant on the run, or to make use of good old women,
evil courtesans, a gluttonous parasite, a braggart soldier,
a changeling, an old man duped by a servant, or even
love, hate, and suspicion? In short, nothing is said that
has not been said before.

—*THE EUNUCH*, PROL., li. 31–41

# Expressions from Roman Poetry

*Horace (65–8 BC)*

## THE GOLDEN MEAN
### *aurea mediocritas*

Whoever is content with the golden mean
Is safe from the squalor
Of a ruined home, and temperately avoids
A house that provokes envy.

—*Odes*, Bk 2, Ode 10, li. 5–8


## SEIZE THE DAY
### *carpe diem*

Be wise, strain your wine, and in this brief space
Cut back long hopes. Even as we speak, envious time
Flees: seize the day, trust little in tomorrow.

—*Odes*, Bk I, Ode 11, li. 6–8

# Expressions from Roman History

## BREAD AND CIRCUSES

Long since, because we can sell our votes to no one,
We have thrown off our cares; those who once bestowed
Rule, the *fasces*, legions, everything, now refrain,
And hunger for only two things:
Bread and circuses.

— JUVENAL, "TENTH SATIRE," li. 78–82

*This phrase is used in a political context to refer to the basic
necessities to keep the people content, to win votes.*

## A PYRRHIC VICTORY

According to some accounts, when one of his men rejoiced
at the victory they had won, Pyrrhus gave this answer:
"If we win another of the price, we are utterly undone."

— PLUTARCH, *LIFE OF PYRRHUS*, CH. 21

*A victory whose cost is so great as to negate its value is
referred to as Pyrrhic.*

## THE SABINE WOMEN

Many people gathered at Rome, for they were eager to see the new city…Even the Sabines came, and brought their wives and children with them….

When the time had come for the spectacles, and the visitors' eyes and minds were all fixed upon them, then the Romans sprang their plot; upon a given signal, the Roman youths broke out to seize the virgins.

—LIVY, *THE HISTORY OF ROME*, BK I, CH 9

*The Sabines, from the Umbrian region of Italy, were ancestors of the ancient Romans. This scene was said to have occurred during the founding of Rome by Romulus.*

## TO CROSS THE RUBICON

Now when Caesar had overtaken his cohorts at the river Rubicon, which was the utmost boundary of his province, he rested for a while; then, considering how great an enterprise he was undertaking, turned to those who stood next to him and said, "As yet, friends, we are able to turn back; but once we pass over this little bridge, there will be no business but by force of arms and dint of sword."

—SUETONIUS, *THE DEIFIED JULIUS*, PARA. 31

*In modern usage, this phrase refers to an irrevocable decision or an action with far-reaching consequences.*

# ᴵ CAME, ᴵ SAW, ᴵ CONQUERED

Having finished all his wars, Caesar rode in five triumphs: four times in the same month, with a few days between each triumph, after vanquishing Scipio; and once again after he had overcome the children of Pompey…In his Pontic triumph, amidst the pageants and pomp, he caused to be carried before him an inscription of these three words: *Veni, vidi, vici;* and this signified, not the outcome of the war, which other conquerors would have celebrated, but rather his speed in dispatching the war.

—SUETONIUS, *THE DEIFIED JULIUS,* PARA. 37

*Caesar's most famous motto.*

# TO TAKE WITH A GRAIN OF SALT

In the chambers of the great king Mithridaes, Cneius Pompeius discovered in a private notebook, in the king's own hand, the formula for an antidote: two dry nuts, the same number of figs, and twenty leaves of rue ground together, with a grain of salt added; whoever took this on an empty stomach would be harmed by no poison that day.

—PLINY THE ELDER, *NATURAL HISTORY,* BK 23, CH 77

*A cautionary note to take something as doubtful, the phrase is a comment on the effectiveness of Pliny's recipe as an antidote to poison.*

# Gods of Roman Mythology

### Jupiter
The sky god, associated with the Greek god Zeus. Jupiter was seen as the source of Roman civic greatness and military might, and made his opinions known by the use of weather signs, especially thunder and lightning.

### Juno
Jupiter's consort, she was considered responsible for all aspects of women's lives and affairs.

### Janus
The first and oldest of the Roman gods; he guarded entrances and exits, bridges and boundaries. On Roman coins he is portrayed symbolically with two faces.

### Mars
The god of war. Sacrifices were offered to him before and after battles. He was originally an agricultural god and is associated with both the wolf and the woodpecker.

### Minerva
Goddess of the intellect and the arts, associated with the Greek goddess Athena. She was patroness of craftsmen, authors, educators, painters, and schoolchildren.

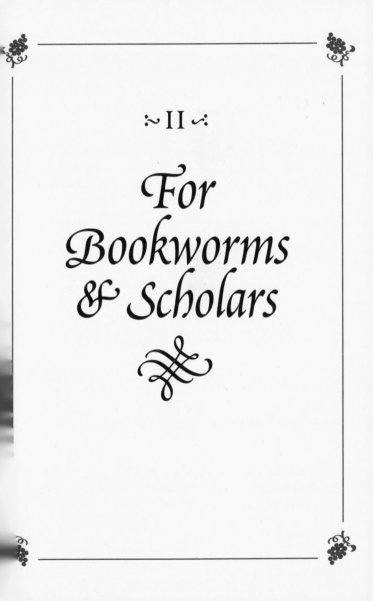

~ II ~

# For Bookworms & Scholars

# Great Latin Authors

### C. Julius Caesar
C. 100–44 BC
Charismatic statesman, strategist, and general, as well as historian.

### C. Valerius Catullus
1ST CENTURY BC
Lyric poet and member of Rome's literary and political élites. His poems primarily describe his unhappy love affair with Clodia (whom he referred to as Lesbia).

### M. Porcius Cato
234–149 BC
Orator, politician, and historian whose manual on farming is the earliest known surviving work in Latin prose.

### M. Tullius Cicero
106–43 BC
Orator, writer, and philosopher. His detailed letters are a crucial source of our knowledge of contemporary Roman life; his rhetorical and philosophical works were highly influential in his time.

## Q. Ennius
239–169 BC
Early Roman poet best known for his epic historical poem the *Annales* and for his tragedies based on Greek drama.

## Horace
65–8 BC
Satirist, critic, and lyric poet.

## D. Junius Juvenalis (Juvenal)
1ST–2ND CENTURY AD
Satirical poet who exposed the decadence of Roman society under Emperor Domitian.

## T. Livius (Livy)
59 BC–AD 17
The Roman Empire's greatest historian, author of the 142-volume *History of Rome*.

## T. Lucretius Carus
1ST CENTURY BC
Poet and Epicurean philosopher whose works include *De Rerum Natura*—literally translated as *On Natural Things*, but concerning legend and mythology.

## P. Ovidius Naso (Ovid)

### 43 BC–C. AD 17

One of ancient Rome's most prolific poets, whose risqué *Ars amatoria* caused Augustus to send him into exile. In addition to love poetry, he wrote on the theme of mythology in *Metamorphoses*.

## Phaedrus

### C. 15 BC–C. AD 50

Author of fables written in verse, which were modelled on Aesop's fables.

## T. Maccius Plautus

### C. 254–184 BC

Dramatist who was the author of more than fifty comedies. Shakespeare's *Comedy of Errors* was based on Plautus's *Menaechmi*.

## C. Plinius Secundus maior (Pliny the Elder)

### C. AD 23–79

Scientist and historian whose surviving works cover natural history, astronomy, and geography. Pliny's curiosity led him to die of asphyxiation watching the eruption of Mount Vesuvius at close range.

### C. Plinius Caecilius Secundus minor (Pliny the Younger)
C. AD 61–110
Prolific letter-writer whose vivid description provides the best surviving account of the eruption of Vesuvius.

### C. Sallustius Crispus (Sallust)
86–C. 34 BC
Historian who wrote in epigrammatic form.

### L. Annaeus Seneca
C. 4 BC–AD 65
Philosopher, playwright (chiefly of tragedies) and essayist.

### Cornelius Tacitus
C. AD 55–120
Orator, statesman, and historian whose works include *Annales*, *Historiae* and *Life of Agricola*.

### P. Vergilius Maro (Virgil)
70–19 BC
Pastoral poet, author of the *Aeneid*, considered the greatest Latin poem.

# Standard Latin Abbreviations

### A.U.C.
*Anno urbis conditae* (reckoned from 753 BC)
from the founding of the city [of Rome]

### A.D.
*Ante diem* (in dates)
Before the day

### COS.
*Consul*
One of the two chief magistrates of the
Roman state under the republic

### E.Q.R.
*Eques Romanus*
the Roman cavalry

### F.
*Filius; fecit*
Son; made by

## G.
*Gallica; Germania*
Pertaining to Gaul; Germany

## H.S.E.
*Hic situs est*
This is the place

## ID.
*Idus*
the Ides—In the Roman calendar,
the 15th day of March, May, July, and October;
the 13th day of the other months

## IMP.
*Imperium, imperator*
Imperial; emperor

## L.
*Locus; libra*
Place; book (as numeral, 50)

## M.
*Mille*
1000

### P.C.

*Patres conscripti*
The senators enrolled
(title of the assembled Senate)

### P.M.

*Pontifex Maximus*
High Priest

### P.P.

*Pater patriae*
The father of the nation

### Q.E.D.

*Quod erat demonstrandum*
That which is demonstrated or proved

### R.P.

*Res publica*
Public affairs

### S.P.Q.R.

*Senatus populusque Romanus*
The Senate and the people of Rome

# Unusual Word Derivations

### ANTLER
from *antocularis*: before the eye

### BUGLE
from *buculus*: a young bull

### CHAPEL
from *capella*: cloak

### PAY
from *pacare*: to make peace

### SOLDIER
from *solidus*: a gold coin

### SULLEN
from *solus*: alone

### VILLAIN
from *villanus*: farm hand

# Scholarly Usage

**AD LIB.**
*ad libitum*, at will

**AD LOC.**
*ad locum*, at the place

**BIBL.**
*bibliotheca*, library

**C./CA.**
*circa*, about; approximately

**CF.**
*confer*, compare

**CON.**
*contra*, against

**E.G.**
*exempli gratia*, for example

**ETC.**
*et cetera*, and so forth

**FL.**
*floruit*, flourished

**IBID.**
*ibidem*, in the same place

**I.E.**
*id est*, that is

**M.M.**
*mutatis mutandis*, necessary changes being made

**MS/MSS**
*manuscriptum, -a*, manuscript(s)

**N.B.**
*nota bene*, take careful note

**OP. CIT.**
*opere citato*, in the work cited

**PASS.**
*passim*, throughout

**Q.V.**
*quod vide*, which see

# Latin Words
# Adopted Directly into English

ADMINISTRATOR

APPENDIX

AQUEDUCT

ATRIUM

AUXILIARY

CENSOR

COHORT

CONSENSUS

CREATOR

CURRICULUM

DICTATOR

EDUCATOR

FORUM

FUROR

GLADIATOR

IBIS

LEGION

LYNX

MAJOR

ODOR

ORATOR

ORCHESTRA

SECTOR

SEPIA

SIMULACRUM

TORPOR

TRIUMVIRATE

TUBA

ULTRA

UXORIOUS

VERNACULAR

VIADUCT

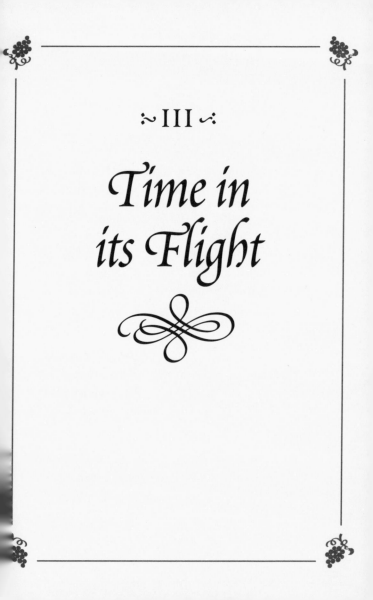

~ III ~

# Time in its Flight

# The Julian Calendar: 46 BC

## January
For Janus, the two-faced god and doorkeeper, who knew the past and foresaw the future. In his shrine, the doors were closed in times of peace and open in times of war.

## February
From *februare*, to expiate or purify, for the mid-month feast of Lupercus, god of fertility. With January, it was added to Rome's original ten-month Alban calendar after 738 BC.

## March
For Mars, the god of war. The wolf, a raiding animal, was sacred to him and closely connected to Rome's legendary founders, Romulus and Remus. During March, the priests of Mars paraded the city with the god's sacred shield.

## April
From *Aperio*, I open, for the springtime burgeoning of nature, regarded as the true beginning of the year in agricultural societies.

## May
Linked both to Maia, the goddess of growth and increase, and *Maiores*, the senate in Rome's original constitution.

## June
For Juno, queen of the gods and guardian of women, which gave rise to the belief that June was the most auspicious month for marriages.

## July
For Julius Caesar (Gaius Julius), who reformed the Roman calendar with advice from the astrologer Sosigenes (by their era, it was about three months ahead of the schedule fixed by the seasons).

## August
For Augustus (Octavian), Julius Caesar's adopted son and the first Roman emperor (27 BC). His reign marked the beginning of the *Pax Romana*, or Roman Peace, which lasted for 200 years.

## September, October, November, & December
Named for their numerical order in the original ten-month calendar as the year's seventh, eighth, ninth, and tenth months.

# The Seasons

The Romans adopted their explanation for the change from winter to summer from the Greeks, changing the names of the principal characters according to their own mythology:

## Ceres
The goddess of agriculture had a home on Mount Olympus but preferred her cottage on Earth, from which she sowed the seeds in springtime, oversaw the growth of grain and fruit all summer, and blessed the harvests in the fall.

## Proserpina
Ceres' beautiful daughter had charge of all the flowers, which sprang up in her footsteps wherever she walked. She tended them with her companions and gathered them for wreaths.

## Pluto

The dour god of the underworld kidnapped Proserpina from her fields and took her to his dark subterranean world to be his wife. She pined there while Ceres searched the Earth for her and appealed for help to the other gods.

## Mercury

The gods' wing-footed messenger traveled to Pluto's realm to announce that the Fates had decreed that Proserpina could return to the light of day only if she had eaten nothing underground. He was grieved to hear that Proserpina had eaten a few of the seeds of a pomegranate.

## The Fates

The arbiters of destiny relented and decreed that Proserpina could return to her mother on Earth for two-thirds of the year but must spend the rest of her time in the underworld. Thus no flowers bloomed and no seeds sprouted during the winter months of her exile.

# Timely Words and Phrases

### Ab ovo usque ad mala
From the beginning to the end (of the feast):
**From the egg to the apples**

### Ad infinitum
Endlessly: **infinity**

### Ad tempus
For the time being: **temporary**

### Aeternus
Everlasting: **eternal**

### Annus
A year (a circuit of the sun): **annual**

### Centesimus
The hundredth: **centennial**

## Dictum factum
**No sooner said than done**

## Dies
Day: **daily**

## Diu
By day: **diurnal**

## Exigua pars est vitae quam nos vivimus
**The part of life we really live is short** (Seneca)

## Ex post facto
After the fact

## Festina lente
**Make haste slowly** (Augustus)

## Interim
Meanwhile: **interval**

## Luna
The moon: **lunar**

*Meminerunt omnia amantes*
**Lovers remember everything** (Ovid)

*Nox*
Night: **nocturnal**

*Nunc aut nunquam*
**Now or never**

*Post mortem*
After death

*Praemonitus praemunitus*
**Forewarned, forearmed**

*Prima lux*
Dawn: **first light**

*Sol*
The sun: **solar**

*Tempus fugit*
**Time flies**

# Timekeeping

The ancients first told time by the marked-off shadows of trees, which led to the creation of the sundial. To measure time at night or on overcast days, the Romans used the water clock, or *clepsydra*, which was also known to the Egyptians, Greeks, and Chinese. The volume of water flowing from one vessel to another was measured to mark the passage of time, similar to the movement of sand in an hourglass. Roman numerals are still used for the faces of clocks and to record dates on monuments and public buildings.

# Timeline of the Roman Republic and Empire

**753 BC** The founding of Rome; the joining of the Seven Hills of Rome.

**509 BC** Roman Republic era begins.

**60 BC** Julius Caesar, Marcus Crassus and Pompey form the First Triumvirate.

**46 BC** Caesar becomes dictator of Rome.

**27 BC** Augustus Caesar becomes emperor, ending the Republican era.

**AD 79** Pompeii destroyed by eruption of Vesuvius.

**AD 98–117** The Roman Empire reaches its greatest extent during the reign of Trajan.

**AD 284–305** The Roman Empire is divided into Eastern and Western sections during the reign of Diocletian; considered the beginning of the end of the Empire.

**AD 476** Romulus Augustus, last Western emperor, is defeated. The Eastern Empire continues as the Byzantine Empire.

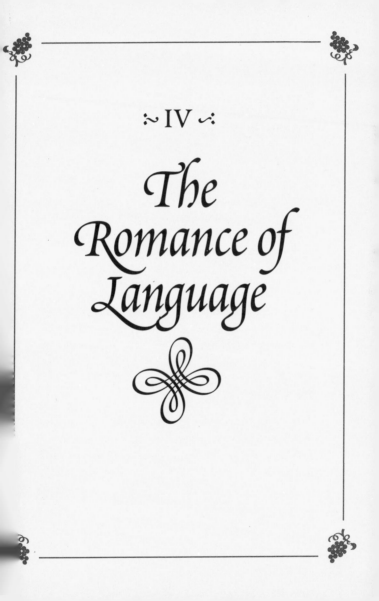

# ~ IV ~

# The Romance of Language

# Expressions and Idioms from Nature

### DOG DAYS

"Who does not know that the solar fires are excited at the rising of the dog-star [Sirius, in August], whose effect is great and is felt on Earth?…Undoubtedly, dogs are most likely to be rabid during the whole of this time."

—Pliny the Elder, *Natural History*

*Pliny's vast encyclopedia in thirty-seven volumes was studded with popular stories—(and errors)—collected on his extensive travels through the Roman Empire, of which the following is an example:*

### IN A NUTSHELL

"There are examples of sharpness of vision that are quite incredible. Cicero reports that there was a copy of Homer's *Iliad* [24 books] inscribed on a piece of parchment enclosed in a nutshell."

## A RARE BIRD

Is there no one among these crowds who
 seems deserving to you?
Let her be beautiful, becoming, rich, and
 fertile; let her place
Ancient ancestors in her galleries;
 let her be more chaste
Than all the Sabine women, with disheveled hair,
 who broke off the war:
A rare bird, as rare on Earth as a black swan;
Who could bear a wife so possessed of
 all things?

　　　　　　　　　—Juvenal, *Sixth Satire*

*Black swans were unknown to the Romans, so when Juvenal
wrote "rare," he meant nonexistent.*

## ANOTHER RARE BIRD

A Happy Man Is Rarer Than a White Crow.

*This popular saying was rendered:* Felix ille tamen corvo
quoque rarior albo.

## TO LEAD BY THE NOSE

"The only certain ground for discovering truth is the faculty of discriminating false from true, distinguishing the sound and genuine from the base and counterfeit, as the silver assayers do with coins. When you have at last managed to acquire such a faculty, then you may investigate the [Stoic] doctrines. Otherwise, I can assure you, you will be led by the nose by anyone who chooses to do it, and you will run after anything they hold out to you, as cattle do after a green bough."

—LUCIAN, *HERMOTIMUS*

## A SNAKE IN THE GRASS

*A dialogue between two rustic poets, which Virgil used to attack his critics, Bavius and Maevius, and to flatter his patron, Pollio:*

DAMOETAS  May he who loves you, Pollio, come to share in our fame; Let honey flow, and the harsh bramble-bush yield balsam.

MENALCAS  Let him, Maevius, that does not hate Bavius, love your songs, And let him also yoke foxes and milk the he-goats.

**DAMOETAS** May you who gather flowers and strawberries from the ground, Flee, you children, from the cold snake hiding in the grass.

—"THIRD ECOLOGUE," LINES 88–93

## WATER FROM A STONE

*A dialogue between two slaves, one of whom is in love and needs money:*

**TOXILUS** You can make me your everlasting friend.

**SAGARISO** How?

**TOXILUS** By giving me sixty silver coins so that I may buy her freedom, which I will pay back immediately, in three days' time, or four. Be a true friend and help me out.

**SAGARISO** What arrogance, to dare asking me for so much money! Even if I sold my whole self, I would scarcely get enough to cover it. You're asking for water from a pumice stone that's thirsty itself.

—PLAUTUS, *THE PERSIAN*, ACT 1, SCENE 1

## TO ADD INSULT TO INJURY

A fly bit the bare head of a bald man, who, trying to swat it, gave himself a slap. Then the fly said, laughing, "You would avenge the bite of so small a creature by killing him; and so you would add insult to injury by striking yourself?"…

—PHAEDRUS, "THE BALD MAN AND THE FLY"

## A COUNTRY MOUSE (HORACE) TAUNTS A CITY MOUSE

If it behooves us to live according to nature,
And seeking a site to build a house is our first task,
Then what place could be more splendid than the
    country?…
Even you, amid your varied columns, nurse a forest
And praise a house with a prospect on distant fields.
You may cast out nature with a pitchfork, yet it will
    always return,
And stealthily break through your stupid disdain,
    victorious."

—*EPISTLES*, BOOK 1, EPISTLE 10

## A ROLLING STONE
## GATHERS NO MOSS
Attributed to the Roman actor Pubilius Syrus,
first century BC

## A BLACKBIRD ALWAYS SITS
## CLOSE TO A BLACKBIRD
The antecedent of our "Birds of a Feather
Flock Together"

## BEWARE OF THE SILENT DOG
## AND STILL WATER
Both were dangerous

## AN ASS AT THE LYRE
## LIKE BEES AT GEOMETRY
Two Roman insults

## TO HOLD THE WOLF BY THE EARS
As in "the bull by the horns"

## WITH CLAWS AND BEAK
"Tooth and nail"

## YOU CAN LEAD A HORSE TO WATER, BUT YOU CANNOT MAKE HIM DRINK

From *stultitia est venatum ducere invitas canes* (Plautus)

## NO SMOKE WITHOUT FIRE

*semper flamma fumo proxima* (Plautus)

## TO SWIM AGAINST THE TIDE

From *contra terrentem bracchia dirigere* (Juvenal)

## ALL THAT LIVES COMES FROM THE EGG

*omne vivum ex ovo*

## EVERY CLOUD HAS A SILVER LINING

From *inter vepres rosae nascuntur*

## TO ERR IS HUMAN

*Errare humanum est* (Cicero)

# Figures of Speech from Virgil

*A* sad thing is a wolf in the fold, rain on ripe corn, wind in the trees, the anger of Amaryllis.

As long as rivers shall run down to the sea, or shadows touch the mountain slopes, or stars graze in the vault of heaven, so long shall your honor, your name, your praises endure.

But meanwhile Neptune saw the ocean's waving commotion…and he summoned the winds, by name. "What arrogance is this, what pride of birth, you winds, to meddle here without my sanction, raising all this trouble? I'll—No the waves come first! but listen to me. You are going to pay for this!"

Arms and the man I sing.

Let us die, and rush into the heart of the fight.

The grove of Angita lamented you,
The glassy watered Fuccinus lamented you,
All limpid lakes lamented you.

# Roman Humour

WHEN THE CATS FALL ASLEEP,
THE MOUSE REJOICES
AND LEAPS FROM HIS HOLE
*Dum felis dormit, mus gaudet et exsilit antro*
(The amusing French variation tells us that "When the
cat's away, the mice will dance on the table")

WHAT A WOMAN SAYS TO
HER FOND LOVER SHOULD
BE WRITTEN ON AIR
OR THE SWIFT WATER
*Mulier cupido quod dicit amanti,*
*In vento et rapida scribere oportet aqua*
CATULLUS

THERE'S NOTHING MORE
CONTEMPTIBLE THAN A BALD MAN
WHO PRETENDS TO HAVE HAIR
*Calvo turpius est nihil compto*
MARTIAL

**IF FAME COMES AFTER DEATH,
I'M IN NO HURRY FOR IT**
*Si post fata venit gloria non propero*
MARTIAL

**THERE IS NOTHING SO ABSURD
AS NOT TO HAVE BEEN SAID
BY A PHILOSOPHER**
*Nihil tam absurdum, quod non dictum sit ab aliquo*
CICERO

**THERE IS NOTHING MORE FRIENDLY
THAN A FRIEND IN NEED**
*Nihil homini amico est opportuno amicius*
PLAUTUS

**NOTHING IS SILLIER THAN
A SILLY LAUGH**
*Risu inepto res ineptior nulla est*
CATULLUS

**A BAD VASE DOESN'T BREAK**
*Malum vas non frangitur*

# Traits and Qualities

**BACCHANALIAN**
from Bacchus, god of wine

**BELLICOSE**
from Bellona, goddess of war

**CENSORIOUS**
from the Roman office of Censor of Public Morals

**HERCULEAN**
from Hercules, the hero who won immortality
by strength

**INTEGRITY**
from *integritas*, soundness

**JUNOESQUE**
from Juno, queen of the gods

**LEGAL**
from *legalis*, pertaining to law

## LUCULLAN
from Lucullus, wealthy Roman general and gourmet

## MERCURIAL
from Mercury, swift messenger of the gods

## PATRICIAN
from *patricius*, member of a noble Roman family

## PLEBEIAN
from *plebeius*, common people

## SATURNINE
from Saturn, the gloomy god of agriculture

## SYLVAN
from *sylva*, woods

## STELLAR
from *stella*, star

## UNDULANT
from *unda*, wave

# Latin in the Garden

The Swedish botanist Carolus Linnaeus (18th century) made it possible for gardeners everywhere to do what they like best: talk and write about their favorite plants. His binomial system of classification gave each plant two names: the first, for the genus, is usually Greek; the second, for the species, Latin:

*Achillea ageratifolia*
YARROW

*Baptisia australia*
BLUE WILD INDIGO

*Campanula carpatica*
BELLFLOWER

*Delphinium belladonna*
LARKSPUR

*Filipendula palmata*
MEADOWSWEET

*Gypsophila paniculata*
BABY'S BREATH

*Helleborus niger*
CHRISTMAS ROSE

*Kniphofia*
TRITOMA/RED HOT POKER

*Lavendula angustifolia*
LAVENDER

*Nepeta x faassenii*
CATMINT

*Papaver orientale*
ORIENTAL POPPY

*Stachys byzantian*
LAMB'S EARS

*Veronica latifolia*
SPEEDWELL

*Yucca filamentosa*
YUCCA/DESERT CANDLE

*Finis*